The Story of a Special Day
Volume 249

September

5

The 248th day of the year (249th in leap years).
There are 117 days remaining until the end of the year.

by Michael Dobson

Timespinner
Press

This book is also available in e-book form for Kindle, e-pub
devices, and other formats from your favorite online booksellers.

For more information about the series, about us, or about your
special day, please email us at editor@timespinnerpress.com.

Look for other volumes in *The Story of a Special Day*, coming
often. See www.timespinnerpress.com for details and for the most
recent information.

Table of Contents

For the definition of "O.S.," "CE," and "BCE" used with some dates , see the section "On Names and Dates."

Cover: The Liberty Bell. (Photo: Wade Dunn Jr., CC BY-SA 4.0)

Quote of the Day

"I can't understand why people are frightened of new ideas. I'm frightened of old ones."

John Cage, composer
born September 5, 1912

Today in History

September 5

Detail from "First Continental Congress," Allyn Cox
(Courtesy Architect of the Capitol)

Event of the Day
First Continental Congress

On September 5, 1774, loud peals from Philadelphia's Liberty Bell sounded at the official opening of the First Continental Congress, where delegates from twelve of the thirteen colonies that would soon form the United States of America met to discuss the growing conflict with Great Britain.

The majority of delegates weren't yet ready to support independence, but all were concerned about recent acts of Parliament that became known to Americans as the "Intolerable Acts." These acts (called the "Coercive Acts" by the British) were designed to punish the colonials for the Boston Tea Party and other acts seen as unpatriotic. One act eliminated the right of Massachusetts to self-government and closed the Port of Boston until such time as the colonials paid for the tea destroyed in the Boston Tea Party. Another act moved the trials of British officials accused of crimes in the colonies to Britain, and finally an act permitting the British to house soldiers in private buildings.

While the British hoped these acts would suppress any rebellious impulses among the colonists, the reverse prove to be the case. The First Continental Congress was called so that the colonies could decide on their common response.

Many important leaders were present, including Benjamin Franklin, George Washington, Patrick

Henry, and others. However, these leaders could not agree on a strategy of separating from Britain, and settled instead on establishing an economic boycott of Great Britain. The First Continental Congress ran until October 26, 1774, when it adjourned.

King George III responded with a speech in Parliament condemning Massachusetts, and the situation became increasingly tense. A Second Continental Congress was convened on May 10, 1775, and a little over a year later, on July 2, 1776, passed a Declaration of Independence. (The final wording of the Declaration required two more days of debate, and was ratified on the more famous date of July 4, 1776.)

The Liberty Bell had been rung before and would be rung again. Originally cast in 1752, it cracked when it was first rung. Twice recast, it was used for various public and religious occasions, and for important events, such as the First Continental Congress. It wasn't rung for the opening of the Second Continental Congress because it was undergoing repairs. Historians have concluded that the oft-told story that the Bell was rung on July 4, 1776, is untrue, but on July 8, 1776, when the Declaration was read aloud to the public, bells all over Philadelphia, including the Liberty Bell, were rung.

Today, the Liberty Bell can be found on Philadelphia's Independence Mall in the Liberty Bell Center.

The Boston Tea Party and its aftermath led to the Intolerable Acts.
(Print by Currier and Ives)

The Second Continental Congress eventually voted for
independence (Courtesy US National Archives)

Michael Dobson

The 1666 Great Fire of London, by Rita Greer

What Happened on September 5?

From the creation of great works of engineering and art, to devastating wars and natural disasters, thousands of years of history have left their mark on each and every day of the year. Here are some important events that occurred on September 5. (Items with a photo or illustration are boxed.)

1666 — The **Great Fire of London,** which began Sunday, September 2, 1666, ends after three days. The fire destroyed 13,200 houses, 87 churches, and St. Paul's Cathedral, but amazingly there were only six recorded deaths. Some 70,000 of the 80,000 residents were left homeless.

1698 — Peter the Great (Tsar Peter I of Russia) declares a **tax on beards** as part of his program to modernize and Europeanize his country.

1781 — The **Battle of the Chesapeake,** also known as the Battle of Virginia Capes, a crucial naval battle in the American Revolutionary War, prevents the Royal Navy from reinforcing or evacuating the forces of General Lord Cornwallis at Yorktown, Virginia, thereby forcing Cornwallis to surrender.

Detail from "Battle of Virginia Capes," by V. Zveg
(Courtesy Naval History and Heritage Command)

Olympic Medal winners, light heavyweight boxing competition. Gold medalist Cassius Clay (Muhammad Ali) second from left, on riser.

1882 — The first **Labor Day Parade** in the United States is held in New York City.

1906 — St. Louis University student Bradbury Robinson throws **the first legal forward pass in American football.**

1921 — An early Hollywood scandal breaks out when young actress **Virginia Rappe dies at a party thrown by film star Roscoe "Fatty" Arbuckle.**

1927 — **Walt Disney** and Ub Iwerks release "Trolley Troubles," **the first cartoon featuring their initial star, Oswald the Lucky Rabbit.**

1945 — Soviet cipher clerk Igor Gouzenko defects to Canada, exposing Josef Stalin's efforts to steal Western nuclear secrets. Some historians regard this defection as **the official beginning of the Cold War.**

1960 — **Cassius Clay (later Muhammad Ali) wins the Olympic Gold Medal** in the light heavyweight boxing competition in Rome.

1972 — The **Munich massacre**, an attack during the Summer Olympics by the Palestinian terrorist group Black September, results in the deaths of eleven Israeli athletes as well as a German police officer.

1972 — **Lynnette "Squeaky" Fromme**, a member of the infamous "Manson family," **attempts to assassinate US President Gerald Ford**.

1977 — The **Voyager I space probe**, which would eventually become the first spacecraft to cross into interstellar space, is launched from Cape Canaveral.

1978 — A series of meetings at the US Presidential retreat at Camp David between Egyptian President Anwar Sadat and Israeli Prime Minister Menachem Begin begins, leading to the **Camp David Accords,** signed thirteen days later.

Camp David negotiations begin: Egyptian President Anwar Sadat (left) arrives and is shown around by US President Jimmy Carter (center) and First Lady Rosalyn Carter (right)

Quote of the Day

"Every time that I fill a high office, I create a hundred discontented men and an ingrate."

Louis XIV, King of France
born September 5, 1638

Births
and
Deaths

September 5

Native American war leader Crazy Horse, who triumphed over General George Armstrong Custer at the Battle of Little Big Horn. Crazy Horse died September 5, 1877

Notable September 5 People

With the current world population at about seven billion people, on average about 19 million people also celebrate their birthdays on September 5 — and that isn't counting millions and millions who came before! No matter when you were born, you share your birthday with many special people whose accomplishments (and occasionally embarrassments) have been noted as part of history.

In this section, you'll meet fascinating people who share your birthday. They're organized by what they're famous for, and then in reverse chronological order from most recent to earliest. Those who are shown in photographs or artwork have a box around them. We don't have photos of everyone, so please forgive us if your favorite person is missing.

Some of these people you've heard of, others will be new to you, but they all make up an important part of the reason that September 5 is a truly special day!

Jesse James (left) and his brother Frank James in 1872

Who Was Born on September 5?

Art and Illustration

Cathy Guisewhite, cartoonist who created the long-running comic strip *Cathy*. (1950)

Frank Thomas, member of Walt Disney's "Nine Old Men" team of animators, created many iconic scenes in Disney films. (1912)

Business and Economics

Werner Erhard, developed Erhard Seminars Training (est), which was widely popular in the 1970s and 1980s. (1935)

Paul Volcker, Chairman of the Federal Reserve during the administrations of Presidents Carter and Reagan, credited with ending a period of high inflation. (1927)

Arthur Nielsen, market analyst who developed the Nielsen television ratings, founded ACNielsen Conpany. (1897)

Crime and Punishment

Jesse James, bank and train robber, iconic figure of the American West. (1847)

Government and Law

Claudette Colvin, African-American civil rights pioneer, first person arrested for resisting bus segregation in Montgomery, Alabama. (1955)

John Danforth, American politician, senator from Missouri and Ambassador to the United Nations. (1936)

Sarvepalli Radhakrishnan, scholar and politician, second President of India. (1888)

Louis XIV the Great of France, the "Sun King," ruled France for 72 years and 110 days, the longest reign of any monarch of a major European country. (1638)

Tommaso Campanella, Dominican friar, philosopher, and prisoner. Defended Galileo Galilei in his first trial. (1568)

Date Masamune (伊達政宗), Japanese regional daimyo, known as "the one-eyed dragon" for his missing eye. He frequently appears as a character in Japanese period dramas. (1894)

Abu Hanifa (أبو حنيفة), Iraqi legal philosopher, sometimes called "the Great Imam," developed one of the major schools of Islamic jurisprudence. (702)

Louis XIV, by Hyacinthe Rigaud

Journalism and Letters

Frank Yerby, historical novelist, first African-American writer to become a millionaire from his writing. (1916)

Nicanor Parra, Chilean poet known throughout Latin America. (1914)

Arthur Koestler, author and journalist famous for the novel *Darkness at Noon.* (1905)

Humphrey Cobb, screenwriter and novelist who wrote *Paths of Glory* (filmed by Stanley Kubrick) and the screenplay of the Humphrey Bogart film *San Quentin.* (1899)

Goffredo Mameli, wrote the lyrics to the Italian national anthem, "Il Canto degli Italiani." (1827)

Aleksey Tolstoy, Russian historical dramatist best known for his trilogy beginning with "The Death of Ivan the Terrible." Second cousin to author Leo Tolstoy. (1817)

Music

Dweezil Zappa, rock guitarist and actor, son of Frank Zappa. (1969)

Loudon Wainwright III, folk singer and humorist, best known for his 1972 novelty hit, "Dead Skunk (in the Middle of the Road." (1946)

Freddie Mercury, lead vocalist and co-principal songwriter of the rock band Queen.

Freddie Mercury (Photo: Carl Lender)

John Cage (Photo: Rob Bogaerts)

Al Stewart, Scottish folk-rocker known for his hits "Year of the Cat" and "Time Passages." (1945)

John Stewart, singer-songwriter known as a member of The Kingston Trio and as the writer of the Monkees' hit song "Daydream Believer."

Buddy Williams, Australian country musician known as "the Yodelling Jackaroo." (1918)

John Cage, avant-garde composer best known for his 1952 composition 4'33" and for his long association with choreographer Merce Cunningham. (1912)

Albert "Sunnyland Slim" Luandrew, American blues pianist. (1906)

Anton Diabelli, composer whose waltz was the basis of Beethoven's "Diabelli Variations." (1781)

Johann Christian Bach, sometimes called "the English Bach" for his long residence in London; eleventh and youngest child of Johann Sebastian Bach. Known for his influence on the young Mozart. (1735)

Performing Arts

Rose McGowan, actress who played Paige in the TV series *Charmed*. (1973)

Kristian Alfonso, actress and former figure skater known for her role as Hope Williams Brady on *Days of Our Lives*. (1963)

Michael Keaton, actor whose films include *Night Shift, Mr. Mom, Beetlejuice, Batman, Batman Returns,* and many others. (1951)

Werner Herzog, influential German filmmaker of such films as *Aguirre, the Wrath of God* and *Fitzcarraldo.*

Raquel Welch, actress and sex symbol, known for roles in such films as *One Million Years BC, Fantastic Voyage, Bandolero!,* and *Bedazzled.* (1940)

George Lazenby, played James Bond in 1969's *On Her Majesty's Secret Service.* (1939)

William Devane, actor known for his roles as Greg Sumner on the television series *Knots Landing* and James Heller on *24,* as well as numerous film roles.

Johnny Briggs, English actor known for his long tenure at Mike Baldwin in the soap opera *Coronation Street.* (1935)

Carol Lawrence, stage and television actress, married to Robert Goulet for many years. (1932)

Bob Newhart, stand-up comedian and actor noted for his one-sided telephone calls and for his sitcoms *The Bob Newhart Show* and *Newhart.* (1929)

Jack Valenti, long-time president of the Motion Picture Association of America, developed the MPAA film rating system. (1921)

Raquel Welch (right) with Dean Martin in *Bandolero!* (1968)

Frank Shuster, half of the Canadian comedy duo Wayne and Shuster. (1916)

Stuart Freeborn, make-up designer known for designing the original *Yoda* for the Star Wars films. (1914)

Darryl F. Zanuck, film producer and studio executive, founded 20th Century Fox. (1902)

Sports

Tracy Edwards, British sailor who led an all-female crew in the Whitbread Round the World Yacht Race; first woman to receive the Yachtsman of the Year trophy. (1962)

Bill Mazeroski, MLB second baseman for the Pittsburgh Pirates, elected to the National Baseball Hall of Fame in 2001. (1936)

Archie Jackson, Australian cricketer, youngest player ever to score a Test century. (1909)

Nap Lajoie, MLB second baseman for Philadelphia and Cleveland, called "the best second baseman in the history of baseball," named to the Baseball Hall of Fame in 1937.

John Wisden, English cricketer who founded the *Wisden Cricketers' Almanack.* (1826)

Nap Lajoie (left) with Honus Wagner, 1904

Portrait of Fritz Leiber by Ed Emshwiller, *The Magazine of Fantasy and Science Fiction*, July 1969 issue.

Who Died on September 5?

Food

Justin Wilson, chef and television host known for his Cajun-inspired dishes and for his catch phrase "I gar-on-tee!". (1997)

Journalism and Letters

Bruce Morton, television news correspondent for CBS and CNN, co-anchor of the *CBS Morning News* from 1974 to 1977. (2014)

Fritz Leiber, science fiction and fantasy writer best known for the *Fafhrd and the Gray Mouser* stories, inducted into the halls of fame in science fiction, fantasy, and horror.. Appeared alongside his acting father in such films as 1939's *The Hunchback of Notre Dame.* (1992)

Jane Roberts, self-proclaimed psychic and spirit medium who published the *Seth Material.* (1984)

Military and Politics

Phyllis Schafly, conservative activist particularly known for her opposition to feminism and her campaign against ratification of the Equal Rights Amendment. (2016)

Arthur MacArthur, Jr., American general who served as military governor-general of the Philippines, winner of the Medal of Honor and father of future Medal winner Douglas MacArthur. (1912)

Sarah Emma Edmonds, served as a man in the Union Army during the American Civil War, also served as a spy against the Confederacy. Author of a best-selling memoir, *Nurse, Soldier, and Spy.* (1898)

Crazy Horse (Tȟašúŋke Witkó), Native American war leader of the Oglala Lakota Sioux, victor at the Battle of Little Bighorn. (1877) *(Photo, page 14)*

Music

Frederick "Denny" Greene, member of the singing group Sha Na Na. (2015)

Joe South, singer-songwriter known for his Grammy winning 1970 hit "Games People Play" and his 1972 hit "Rose Garden." (2012)

Georg Solti, conductor, best known for his tenure with the Chicago Symphony Orchestra, won 32 Grammy Awards. (1993)

General Arthur MacArthur, Jr., (center) and staff in 1898

Performing Arts

Hugh O'Brian, American actor known for his roles on the TV series *The Life and Legend of Wyatt Earp* and *Search*, as well as numerous film roles. (2016)

Setsuko Hara (原節子), Japanese actress who appeared in nearly 70 films, best known for her roles in *Late Spring* (1949) and *Tokyo Story* (1953).

Allen Funt, created and hosted the television series *Candid Camera*. (1999)

Leo Penn, film director, father of actor Sean Penn. (1998)

Claude Renoir, French cinematographer, nephew of director Jean Renoir and grandson of painter Pierre-Auguste Renoir. (1993)

Gert Fröbe, actor best known for playing the title role in the James Bond film *Goldfinger*. (1988)

Religion

D. James Kennedy, American televangelist known for his television and radio program *The Coral Ridge Hour/Truth That Transforms*. (2007)

Mother Teresa (Saint Teresa of Calcutta), Roman Catholic nun and missionary, known for her leadership of the Missionaries of Charity, received the Nobel Peace Prize for her work. (1997)

Science and Medicine

Ludwig Boltzmann, Austrian physicist who explained how the properties of atoms determine the physical properties of matter. (1906)

Rudolf Virchow, German physician known as the "father of modern pathology" for his role in bringing science to medicine. (1902)

Auguste Comte, French philosopher who helped found the discipline of sociology, credited with coining the word "altruism" *(altruisme)*. (1857)

Sports

Clem Hill, set a world record of 3,412 runs in Test Cricket, member of the Australian Cricket Hall of Fame. (1945)

Quote of the Day

"I'm possessed by love — but isn't
everybody?"

Freddie Mercury, singer-songwriter
born September 5, 1946

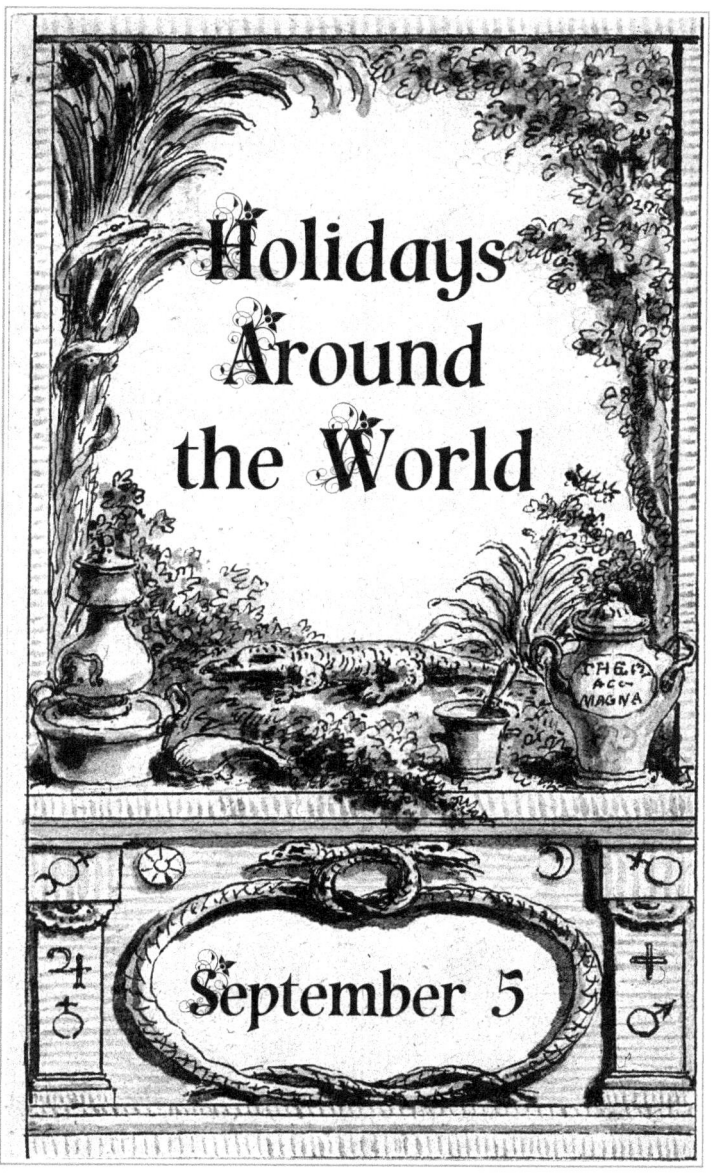

Holidays
Around
the World

September 5

A 1942 Labor Day poster for the US Office of War Information

Holidays Around the World

If you're looking for a reason to take your special day off, you should know that every single day is a holiday somewhere in the world! Here's what you can celebrate on September 5!

Labor Day

Many countries take a day to honor workers, and often take it as a public holiday. Most countries celebrate Labor (sometimes Labour) Day on May 1; the United States and Canada celebrate on the first Monday of September instead.

International Worker's Day (various nations)
The Second International, a conference of communist and socialist parties in 1886, declared May 1 to be International Worker's Day. Because May 1 (May Day) is a public holiday in many nations, it has been adopted as Labor (or Labour) Day in most of the world. *(Always May 1)*

Labor Day (US)/Labour Day (Canada)
Labor Day in the United States and Canada is celebrated on the first Monday of September. This date commemorates a key event in the Canadian labor movement. American labor leaders, witnessing a Canadian Labor Day parade, took the custom back to New York, and it spread through a number of states, anchored to that date.

Labor Day is celebrated today with parades, ceremonies, and public events. It's also known as the unofficial end of the summer season, so last-minute beach trips and back-to-school sales are also popular. *(Varies from September 1-7)*

General Events

International Day of Charity (international)

Declared by the UN General Assembly to promote awareness of charity related activities worldwide, date selected to honor the passing of Mother Teresa. A number of events related to this day also occur on September 5 in various nations and by various organizations. *(Always September 5)*

Food Holidays

In the United States, almost every day of the year is dedicated to a particular food. (Some other countries do this also, but not every day.) Sponsored by manufacturers, retailers, farmers, or simply fans, these days are often proclaimed by the President, Congress, state governors, or mayors. Given that there are more different foods than days of the year, some days honor more than one kind of food!

September 5 is **National Cheese Pizza Day.** According to Foodimentary.com, over 93% of Americans eat at least one pizza a month! Looks like September 5 is a good opportunity to indulge.

In addition, the entire month of September is used to celebrate numerous foods. Here's a list of what to eat in the month of September!

- National Chicken Month
- National Honey Month
- National Mushroom Month
- National Papaya Month
- National Potato Month
- National Rice Month

Christian Feast Days and Holidays

Each day in the year is considered a feast day for one or more saints. They are somewhat different in western Christianity (Catholicism and many forms of Protestantism) and in eastern (Orthodox) Christianity. There are many others; this is a selection.

In *Western Christianity*, it is the feast day of Saints Bertin, Teresa of Calcutta, Genebald of Laon, Gregorio Aglipay (Episcopal Church), and Zechariah and Elisabeth..

In *Eastern Orthodox Christianity*, it is also the commemoration of Saints Herculanus, Quintius, Obdulia, and Victoriunus. (These are observed on August 23 by "Old Calendarists.")

Honorary Months

Presidents, Congresses, and nations around the world issue proclamations recognizing particular months to honor certain causes. These events generally fall in November, though honorary months do come and go. Holidays established by states and nonprofit organizations are listed if verified. If not otherwise specified, all months are US. There is some variation from year to year; some celebratory months get added and others get dropped. Two places to get up to date information are the current edition of *Chase's Calendar of Events* or the website Brownielocks (www.brownielocks.com).

- Baby Safety Month
- Be Kind to Editors and Writers Month
- **Bourbon Heritage Month**
- Children's Good Manners Month
- College Savings Month
- Happy Cat Month
- International Square Dancing Month
- National Recovery Month
- National Service Dog Month
- Responsible Dog Ownership Month

Moveable and Multi-Day Events

Some events take place over a specific week or time period. Start and finish dates may vary from year to year. Some events occur on different days each year (such as "fourth Saturday of a month"). These events sometimes take place on this day.

First Week of September *(begins September 1-7)*

- International Enthusiasm Week
- National Nutrition Week (UNICEF/India)
- National Payroll Week
- Substitute Teacher Appreciation Week

Thursday following the first Sunday of September *(any day, September 5-11)*

- *Jeûne genevois* (Genevan fast), public holiday in the canton of Geneva, Switzerland.

A glass and bottle of bourbon, for Bourbon Heritage Month
(Photo: Dirk Ingo Franke)

Quote of the Day

"We have the power to transform the quality of our lives."

Werner Erhard, founder of est
born September 5, 1935

About
the
Month
of

CHEI. P.
ACC
MAGNA

September

September, from the *Brevarium Grimani* by Simon Bening (c.1510)

September: The Ninth Month

The morrow was a bright September morn;
The earth was beautiful as if new-born;
There was that nameless splendor everywhere,
That wild exhilaration in the air,
Which makes the passers in the city street
Congratulate each other as they meet.

Henry Wadsworth Longfellow, "Tales of a Wayside Inn"

In Latin, *septem* means "seven," so it may seem strange that September is actually the *ninth* month of the year. The original Roman calendar, on which ours is based, started in March, making September indeed the seventh month. No one is completely sure when the start of the year was moved to January, but the traditional name of September stuck.

Romans also associated September with the god Vulcan, and thus expected the month to have fires, volcanic eruptions, and earthquakes.

In the northern hemisphere, September marks the beginning of meteorological autumn. In the southern hemisphere, September is the seasonal equivalent of March, the beginning of spring.

September and December always begin on the same day of the week. However, no other month in the same year will end on the same day of the week as September.

For countries that switched from the Julian to the Gregorian calendars in 1752, the date jumped from September 2 to September 14, meaning that there is no September 12 in that year.

September in Other Cultures

In Old English, the month of September was known as *Hāligmōnaþ*. Anglo-Saxons called it *Gerst monath* (Barley month) celebrating the barley harvest that would shortly be turned into beer. In Finland, it is *syyskuu*, in Poland *wrzesień*, and in Greece *Σεπτέμβριος*. The Russians call the month *сентябрь*. While both the Hebrew and Arabic cultures have their own calendar system, the Hebrew word for "September" is ספטמבר and in Arabic it's سبتمب. The Azerbaijani call the month *Sentyabr*. In Hindi, the month of "sitambar" is written सितंबर. In both China and Japan, it's known as 九月, 구월 in Korea, and 腩尬 in Vietnam.

September Sayings and Superstitions

Here are some wedding sayings and superstitions associated with the month of September.

- "Marry in September's shrine, your living with be rich and fine."
- "A September bride will be discreet, affable, and much liked."
- "Married in September's golden glow / Smooth and serene your life will go."

As for which day of the week, that's easy.

Monday for health, Tuesday for wealth,
Wednesday best of all, Thursday for losses,
Friday for crosses, Saturday for no luck at all.

September Symbols

Birthstone: Sapphire, representing clear thinking.

Star sapphire

Birth Flowers: Forget-me-not, morning glory, and aster.

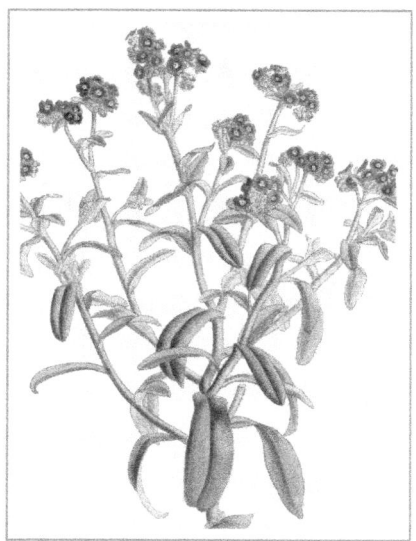

Forget-me-not (*moyosotis azorica*)

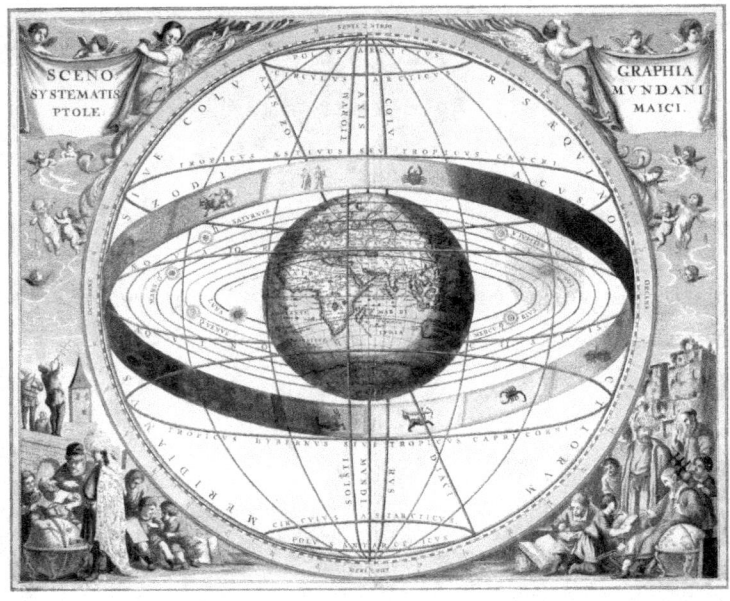

Scenography of the Ptolemaic Cosmography, by Johannes van Loon, based on Andreas Cellarius's *Harmonia Macrocosmica,* 1660

September 5 Zodiac Signs

From the perspective of someone on Earth, the Sun appears to move through the sky throughout the year, along a path astronomers call the *ecliptic plane*. The ecliptic plane is divided into twelve constellations, known as the zodiac, based on traditionally observed patterns of stars. On your birthday, you can't see your constellation, because it's in the daytime sky.

The zodiac was first developed by Babylonian astronomers about 2,500 years ago. Because they were unaware that the Earth wobbles like a spinning top (known as *precession*), they didn't make allowance for the fact that the Sun's path through the zodiac changes over time.

That means there are now two sets of dates for your birth sign. The *tropical dates* are the original Babylonian dates; the *sidereal dates* tell you where the Sun actually appears as it moves along its annual path.

For September 5, the tropical signs is **Virgo** and the sidereal sign is **Leo**.

Leo

Tropical July 23 to August 23
Sidereal August 16 to September 15

In Greek mythology, Leo, the lion, was killed by Hercules during one of his twelve labors. The easiest part of Leo to see in the night sky is an asterism known as the Sickle, looking a bit like a backward question mark. One of the nearest stars to Earth, Wolf 359 (just under eight light-years away), can be found in Leo.

In astrology, Leo is considered to be a fire sign. Traits associated with Leo are generosity, warmth, brightness, and self-motivation. Leos are supposed to be compatible with Aries and Sagittarius, and to a lesser extent with Gemini, Libra, and Aquarius.

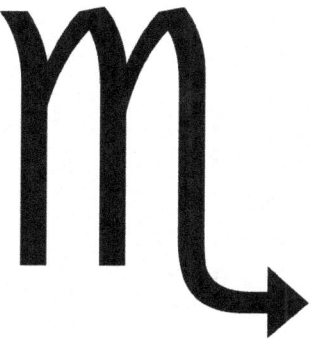

Virgo

Tropical August 23 to September 22
Sidereal September 16 to October 15

The constellation Virgo is the second-largest constellation in the night sky. Its brightest star, Spica, makes it easy to locate. If you can find the Big Dipper (Ursa Major), follow the curve in the Dipper's handle. The second bright star you see is Spica.

In Greek and Roman mythology, Virgo is associated with Demeter (Ceres), the goddess of wheat, and also with Erigone and Astraea. In astrology, Virgo is known as a "mutable sign." It's associated with being reflective and receptive to the ideas of others, sensitive to criticism, and oriented toward detail and precision.

Virgos are supposed to be compatible with Capricorn, Taurus, Cancer, and Scorpio, and to a lesser extent with Virgo and Pisces.

Illustration by Edward Penfield

What Day of the Week is September 5?

On what day of the week does September 5 fall?

Surprisingly, this isn't an easy question. Because the calendar year is 365 days long (366 in leap years), it doesn't divide evenly by the seven days of the week.

Also, the Earth goes around the Sun in about 365-1/4 days, so a calendar tends to drift over time. That's why the same date falls on different weekdays in different years.

This is made even more complicated by a change in calendars that took place in 1582. Our modern calendar has its roots in ancient Rome, in a calendar reform conducted by Julius Caesar. Caesar commissioned mathematicians to attack the problem, and they came up with the idea of leap years, and thus standardized the calendar for centuries to come. This was called the Julian calendar.

Over time, however, the small errors in Caesar's calculation compounded. That's why Pope Gregory XIII commissioned the Gregorian calendar, used in most of the world today. Some countries converted in 1582, when the calendar was first developed; some converted later; other still haven't changed.

Gregorian and Julian aren't the only types of calendars. The Hebrew year, the Islamic year, and many other calendars are used in different parts of the world and among different people.

You can convert Gregorian dates to other calendars, including the Hebrew calendar, the Islamic calendar, and even the Mayan calendar by visiting the Fourmilab Calendar Converter at http://www.fourmilab.ch/documents/calendar/.

Chinese calendar systems are quite complex and have changed several times; a full discussion is far beyond the scope of this book. If you're interested, you can find information here: http://www.hermetic.ch/cal_stud/chinese_cal.htm.

On Names and Dates

Historians use "CE" (Common Era) and "BCE" (Before the Common Era) instead of the more common "AD" (Anno Domini, or Year of Our Lord) and "BC" (Before Christ), reflecting the fact that the year-numbering system established by the Gregorian calendar is used throughout the world in many countries not culturally Christian.

The CE/BCE designation dates back to at least 1708, and has been adopted as a standard by the United Nations and the Universal Postal Union. Because this series of books covers events and people of all nations and cultures, we use the CE/BCE terms.

The abbreviation "O.S." ("Old Style") on some dates refers to the fact that the Russian Empire did not switch from the Julian to the Gregorian calendar at the same time as the rest of Europe, and therefore some figures and events have two dates.

Also, in the Julian calendar in England in the 16th century, the year began on March 25 rather than January 1. To avoid confusion with Gregorian dates, dates between January and March were often written using both years.

People and events whose original names are not in the Western alphabet have their native names (where possible) in the appropriate script shown in parenthesis. If you are using an e-reader to access an electronic version of this book, all characters don't always display on all devices.

A 50-year brass perpetual calendar.

Quote of the Day

"Time is an illusion, lunchtime doubly so."

Douglas Adams,
from *The Hitchhiker's Guide to the Galaxy*

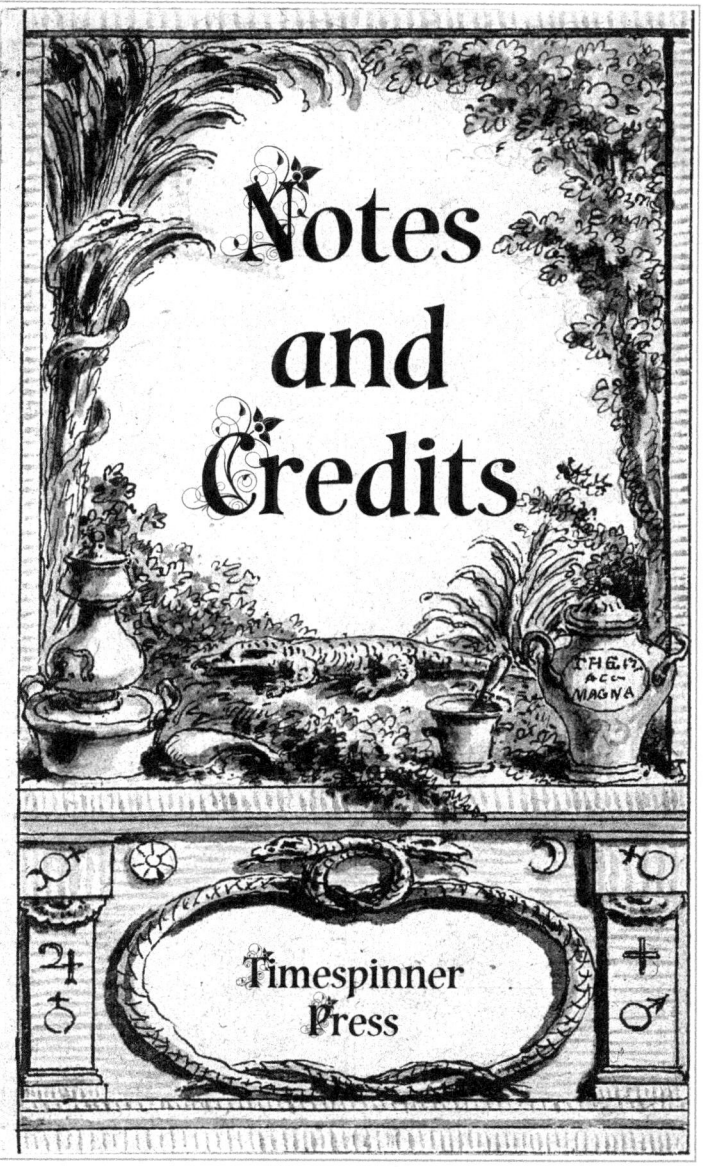

Notes
and
Credits

THEI₂
ACC
MAGNA

Timespinner
Press

Cartoon by John T. McCutcheon

Copyright, Credit, and Contact

Follow Us

Our blog "This Day in History" (http://timespinnerpress.com/this-day-in-history/) features short articles on events and people associated with each day, and updates several times each week. Also subscribe to the "Quote of the Day" at http://timespinnerpress.com/quote-of-the-day/. You can get daily links by following us on Facebook at TimespinnerPress, or on Twitter as @sidewisethinker.

Contact Us

Find an error or a format problem? Want information about the series, about us, or about when the volume for your special day might be available? Please email us at editor@timespinnerpress.com. (We also take requests if your special day isn't yet complete. Please give us at least six weeks' notice if possible.)

Sources

We owe a great debt to Wikipedia, which is our first stop for research. We attempt to make independent confirmation of all important dates and facts through a variety of other sources.

Other sources we frequently use include the Library of Congress; "on this day" listings from *Encyclopedia Britannica*, the *New York Times*, and the BBC; Omniglot for the names of months in other languages; *Chase's Calendar of Events*; and, of course, the always essential Google.

All art and photographs are either in the public domain, used under a Creative Commons license, or with a "fair use" justification, and most frequently come from Wikimedia Commons and the Library of Congress Prints and Photographs Division.

Attribution is provided where possible, or as requested by the copyright owner, or when there is particular historical significance, listed below. For information about any particular illustration or photograph, please contact us.

Credits

1. The cover photograph of the Liberty Bell was taken in 2015 by Wade Dunn Jr. It is used here under CC BY-SA 4.0 International.

2. The illustration of the month of September used on the back cover is from the French Gothic illuminated manuscript *Les Très Riches Heures du duc de Berry* by the Limbourg Brothers, Jean Colombe, and an intermediate painter whose name is lost to history. It is in the public domain because its copyright has expired.

3. The box graphic used on the first page is from a 1916 pamphlet entitled "Divorce versus Democracy" authored by G. K. Chesterton, originally published in London by the Society of St. Peter and St. Paul. It is in the public domain in the US because it was published prior to 1923, and is in the public domain in all countries (including the country of origin) in which the copyright time is the author's life plus 70 years or less.

4. The graphic design for the section pages in this book is from a design originally created for a pharmacy label. It is courtesy of Wellcome Images (ICV No 11073, photo V0010813), and is used here under CC BY-SA 4.0.

5. The painting of the First Continental Congress by Allyn Cox is in the collection of the United States Capitol. It is in the public domain as a work created by an employee of the Architect of the Capitol as part of that person's official duties. The image has been cropped.

6. The 1846 Currier and Ives print of the Boston Tea Party is in the public domain because its copyright has expired.

7. The illustration from the Second Continental Congress is in the public domain as a work created by an employee of the US federal government as part of that person's official duties.

8. The 2008 painting of the Great Fire of London is by Rita Greer, who made the work freely available under the terms of the Free Art License. The image has been cropped.

9. The 1962 painting "Second Battle of the Virginia Capes" by V. Zveg is in the public domain as a work created by an employee of the US military as part of that person's official duties. The original can be found in the Hampton Roads Naval Museum, Norfolk, Virginia. Photo: US Naval History and Heritage Command, NH-73927-KN. The image has been cropped.

10. The 1960 photograph of medal winners of the light heavyweight boxing category was taken by the Polish Press Agency. It is in the public domain under Art. 3 of copyright law of March 29, 1926 of the Republic of Poland and Art. 2 of copyright law of July 10, 1952 of the People's Republic of Poland, all photographs by Polish photographers (or published for the first time in Poland or simultaneously in Poland and abroad) published without a clear copyright notice before the law was changed on May 23, 1994 are assumed public domain in Poland.

11. The photograph of Anwar Sadat's arrival at Camp David is in the public domain as a work created by an employee of the Executive Office of the President as part of that person's official duties. It is courtesy of the US National Archives, NAIL Control Number NLC-WHSP-C-07256-18A.

12. The 1877 photograph of Crazy Horse is in the public domain because its copyright is expired. (The authenticity of this photograph has been disputed.)

13. The 1872 photograph of Jesse and Frank James is in the public domain because its copyright has expired. It is courtesy of the US Army Corps of Engineers Digital Visual Library.

14. The 1701 portrait of Louis XIV is by Hyacinthe Rigaud, and can be found in the collection of the Prado. It is in the public domain because its copyright has expired.

15. The 1977 photograph of Freddie Mercury is by Carl Lender, and is used here under CC BY-SA 2.0.

16. The 1988 photograph of John Cage was taken by Rob Bogaerts. It is from the Anefo photo collection in the Dutch National Archives, and is used here under CC BY-SA 3.0 Netherlands.

17. The publicity photograph from the 1968 film *Bandolero!* is in the public domain because it was first published in the United States between 1923 and 1977 without a copyright notice. Typically, publicity photographs are not copyrighted because of the way in which they are intended to be used.

18. The 1904 photograph of Napoleon Lajoie and Honus Wagner is in the public domain because its copyright has expired. The photo is in the collection of the Boston Public Library.

19. The 1969 cover from *The Magazine of Fantasy and Science Fiction* by Ed Emshwiller is copyrighted by the magazine publisher. It is used here under "fair use" provisions of the copyright code in a low-resolution and reduced format version to show Fritz Leiber as a major fantasy and science fiction writer; no equivalent free media exists.

20. The 1898 photograph of General Arthur MacArthur, Jr., and staff is from the collection of the US National Archives, ARC 524382. It is in the public domain because its copyright has expired. The photograph has been cropped.

21. The 1942 Labor Day poster was created for the Office of Emergency Management, Office of War Information, and is in the public domain as a work created by an employee of the US government as part of that person's official duties. It is in the collection of the US National Archives, NAIL Control No. NWDNS-208-COM-141.

22. The 2015 photograph of a glass and bottle of bourbon whiskey is by Dirk Ingo Franke, and is used here under CC BY-SA 4.0 International.

23. The painting "September" is from the *Brevarium Grimani*, circa 1510, and is in the public domain because its copyright has expired.

24. The photograph of a star sapphire was released into the public domain by its author, Mitchell Gore.

25. The chromolithograph of a forget-me-not is by Louis-Aristide Léon Constans and originally appeared in the 1852-1853 edition of *Paxton's Flower Garden*. It is in the public domain because its copyright has expired.

26. The celestial sphere is from *Scenography of the Ptolemaic Cosmography*, by Johannes van Loon, based on Andreas Cellarius's *Harmonia Macrocosmica*, 1660. It is in the public domain because its copyright has expired.

27. The 1906 automobile calendar is by Edward Penfield, and is in the collection of the Library of Congress Prints and Photographs Division. It is in the public domain because its copyright has expired.

28. The 50-year perpetual calendar photograph is in the public domain.

29. The cartoon by John T. McCutcheon is from his 1905 collection *The Mysterious Stranger and Other Cartoons by John T. McCutcheon*. It is in the public domain because its copyright has expired.

License Description and Terms

Aside from material purely in the public domain, photographs and other material in this book are used under specific licenses permitting free use, usually with an attribution requirement. For full text and terms of these licenses, click or enter the appropriate links below. If you believe there is an error in the copyright status or attribution of any of these images, please email us.

- Creative Commons Attribution 2.0 Generic (CC-BY 2.0): http://creativecommons.org/licenses/by/2.0/deed.en

- Creative Commons Attribution-Share Alike 3.0 Generic (CC-BY-SA 3.0): http://creativecommons.org/licenses/by-sa/3.0/

- Creative Commons Attribution-Share Alike 2.5 Generic (CC-BY-SA 2.5): http://creativecommons.org/licenses/by-sa/2.5/deed.en

- Creative Commons Attribution-Share Alike 2.0 Generic (CC-BY-SA 2.0): http://creativecommons.org/licenses/by/2.0/deed.en

- Creative Commons Attribution-Share Alike 1.0 Generic (CC-BY-SA 1.0): http://creativecommons.org/licenses/by-sa/1.0/deed.en

- CC0 1.0 Universal (CC0 1.0) Public Domain Dedication (CC0 1.0) http://creativecommons.org/publicdomain/zero/1.0/deed.en

- GNU Free Documentation License (GFDL): http://en.wikipedia.org/wiki/Wikipedia:Text_of_the_GNU_Free_Documentation_License

- License Art Libre (Free Art License): http://artlibre.org

Timespinner
Press

Other Books from Timespinner Press

The Story of a Special Day
Michael Dobson

A series of (eventually) 366 volumes covering everything that happened on your special day! Events, births, deaths, quotes, holidays, and much more. It's like a birthday card they'll never throw away!

US$7.95 print / US$2.99 ebook.

From Plassey to Pakistan
Humayun Mirza

The history of British Colonial India and the formation of Pakistan from the unique perspective of the son of Pakistan's first president and last of the royal line of Bengal, Bihar, and Orissa! This unique historical document tells the inside story of this distinguished family, including the detailed story of the coup that toppled his father from power!

US$27.95 print

A Whole New Navy: America's War in the Pacific

Miles Durr

The most comprehensive and detailed description of America's naval war in the Pacific ever—every battle, every ship, every task force and every task group from Pearl Harbor through the Japanese surrender! A must-have for the collection of every World War II buff!

US$29.95 print

Improbable History: The Weird, the Obscure, and the Strangely Important

edited by Michael Dobson

From the birth of Western civilization to the rescue of Apollo 13, from the Leaning Tower of Pisa to Florence's Duomo, history has often turned on small, improbable details. Whatever happened to the ancient Samaritan people? Why did a fortuitous rainstorm allow the British to conquer India? How did an air raid in Italy lead to the development of chemotherapy? What happened when Albert Einstein met Adolf Hitler on the streets of Berlin? How did the Japanese manage to attack the US mainland using balloons? A cast of award-winning writers tackle some of the strangest tales in history!

US$19.95 print